AF481072

A CHILD'S GUIDE TO CAPITALISM

SOCIAL STUDIES BOOK GRADE 6

CHILDREN'S GOVERNMENT BOOKS

Speedy Publishing LLC

40 E. Main St. #1156

Newark, DE 19711

www.speedypublishing.com

Copyright 2017

In this book, we're going to talk about capitalism. So, let's get right to it!

WHAT IS CAPITALISM?

If a nation has a capitalistic economy, it means that private individuals can own property. In a capitalistic society, the government doesn't own everything. For example, let's say you want to go to the grocery store to buy something. You can go to any store you want and buy from any merchant. You can make your own choice about who to buy from.

Also, if you buy a piece of property, such as a house or a piece of land, it belongs to you. Not all governments operate this way. In some countries, individuals are not allowed to own land at all. The government owns all the land and private individuals can't own their own property.

For example, in a communistic system the government controls all the land and businesses.

This type of economy is described as a "command" economy because the citizens are commanded what to do.

WHAT DOES THE TERM "FREE MARKET" MEAN?

If you want something, you either need to barter for it or work so you can earn the money to purchase it. When you live in a capitalistic country, you can buy from someone or sell to someone without the government restricting your activities as long as it's something that's legal to buy or sell.

永興隆 國康
窗簾 · 布藝 · 床上用品
www.homestyle.com.hk
寶寶布藝
BO BO DECO
樂善髮型設計
Harmony Hair Design
樂蕙髮
剪髮

Most countries that have capitalism aren't completely "free" economies. The government does some regulation and so do trade unions. Because of this, the United States is a "mixed economy." For example, if the stock market begins to crash, the United States government has regulations that prevent a total collapse of the economy.

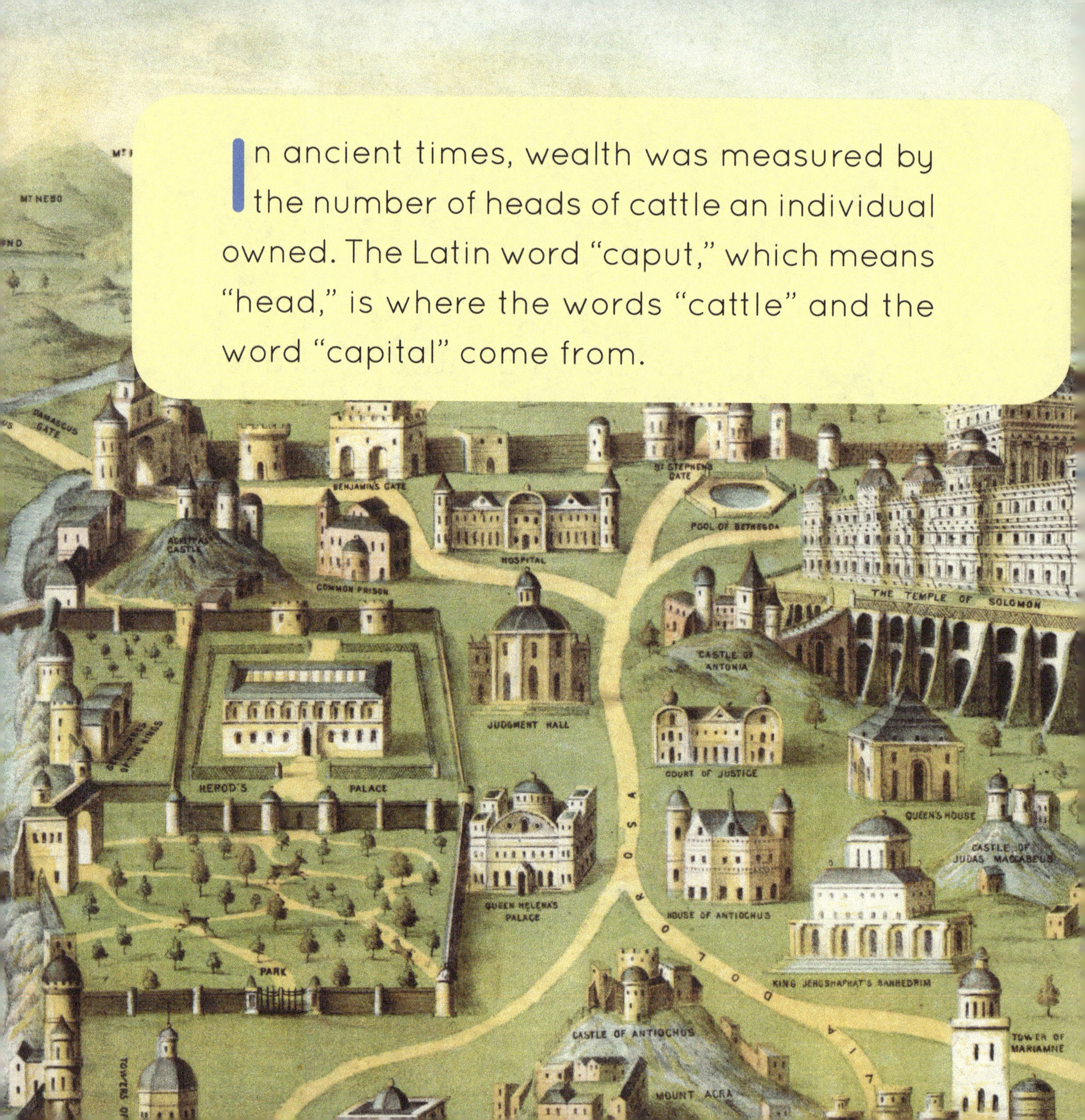

In ancient times, wealth was measured by the number of heads of cattle an individual owned. The Latin word "caput," which means "head," is where the words "cattle" and the word "capital" come from.

CHURCH OF ASCENSION
BETHANY
MOUNTAINS OF ARABIA
CHRIST TAUGHT HIS DISCIPLES TO PRAY
TOMB OF ST JAMES
ABSALOM'S PILLAR
ZACHARIAH'S TOMB
KIDRON
THE TEMPLE OF CHEMOSH
KING'S GARDEN OLIVET
VALLEY OF HINNOM
IDOL MOLECH
CHRIST RIDING INTO JERUSALEM
ISAIAH'S TOMB
KING MANASSEH'S TOMB
KING MANASSEH'S GARDEN
WELL OF THE VIRGIN
TOPHET
THE STONE ZOHELETH
WELL OF ENROGEL
TO THE DEAD SEA
ACELDAMA
THE POTTERS FIELD
BEAUTIFUL GATE
ORPHEL
WATER GATE
EZRA
TREE OF ISAIAH
WATERGATE ST.
FOUNTAIN
SILOAM
HOUSE OF ANNAS THE HIGH PRIEST
KING'S FISH POOL
STREET
CAESAR'S PALACE
TOWN HOUSE
GATE
PALACE OF CAIAPHAS THE HIGH PRIEST
RECORDS
SCHOOL HOUSE
THE HOUSE OF THE MIGHTY
KING'S PALACE
KING DAVID & SOLOMON'S SEPULCHRES
OF ST PETER
ZION'S GATE
KING'S GARDEN

This type of "capital" doesn't relate to a capital city. Instead, it just means something that has a value that everyone recognizes.

Money that can be invested is one type of financial capital and so is any type of property that has value, such as jewelry. In fact, anything that others recognize has value and can be used to create wealth is capital.

Some inventors have patents that are valuable and that they can use to create wealth so these patents are a form of capital. Manufacturing equipment, such as tools and machinery, and real estate are also valuable assets that can create wealth so they are considered capital too.

MANUFACTURING EQUIPMENT

SUPPLY
DEMAND

SUPPLY AND DEMAND

One of the basic principles of capitalism is that supply as well as demand goes hand in hand and these two situations will impact price. Imagine you wanted to buy one of Leonardo da Vinci's inventor's journals. He didn't write too many of these and Leonardo is very famous so one of his journals would be worth a lot of money.

Because of Leonardo's fame and the fact that it's a rare item, one of his inventor's journals would not only be worth a lot, it would be a good investment since no more of these journals could be produced. The billionaire Bill Gates bought one of these, called the Codex Leicester, for $30.8 million dollars.

BILL GATES

ow imagine you're a budding inventor and you want to write your own inventor's journal. You go to the office supply store and you see piles and piles of blank journals on the shelf. The price for this journal might be $1.75. That's because there are tons of them around.

ots of supply of a product that everyone has means the price goes down. Of course, if you fill it with valuable sketches of future inventions and you become

famous, your journal may someday be valuable too. So, supply and demand will set the price in a capitalistic economy. The government doesn't fix the price.

ADAM SMITH

ADAM SMITH AND "THE WEALTH OF NATIONS"

In 1776, a Scottish philosopher called Adam Smith published a book that is commonly known as "The Wealth of Nations." In this book, he described his theories concerning an economy that would operate on a "free market" basis.

He was describing the principles of capitalism, even though the word "capitalism" wasn't part of the language until more than 100 years after the book was published.

BUY OR
LEASE

BUY, SELL, WORK, HIRE

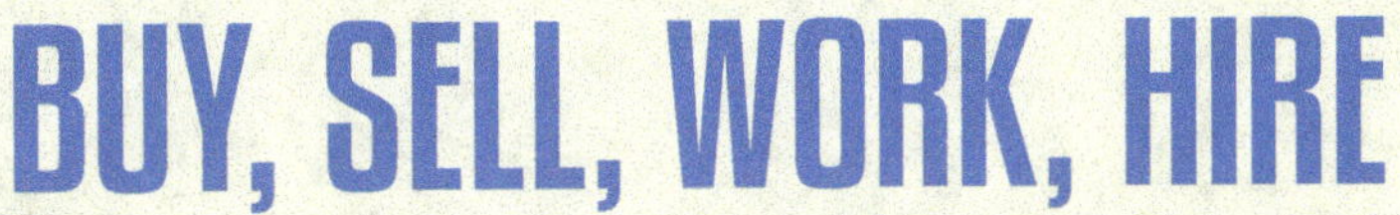

In a capitalistic system, people can choose to sell or lease their property to someone else. You can buy, lease, or borrow something from someone else.

The government doesn't regulate these transactions. You can buy or sell without getting permission from anyone.

BUY
BUY
BUY
SELL
SELL
SELL

You can also choose to hire whomever you want as long as they are qualified to do a job and they accept the pay and benefits you offer.

BUSINESSMAN

You may have heard of the term "venture capitalists." Venture capitalists are people who invest in companies that are just starting. They invest in these companies and when the companies turn a profit, the investment is paid back with interest. Anyone who supports and believes in the system of capitalism can be described as a capitalist.

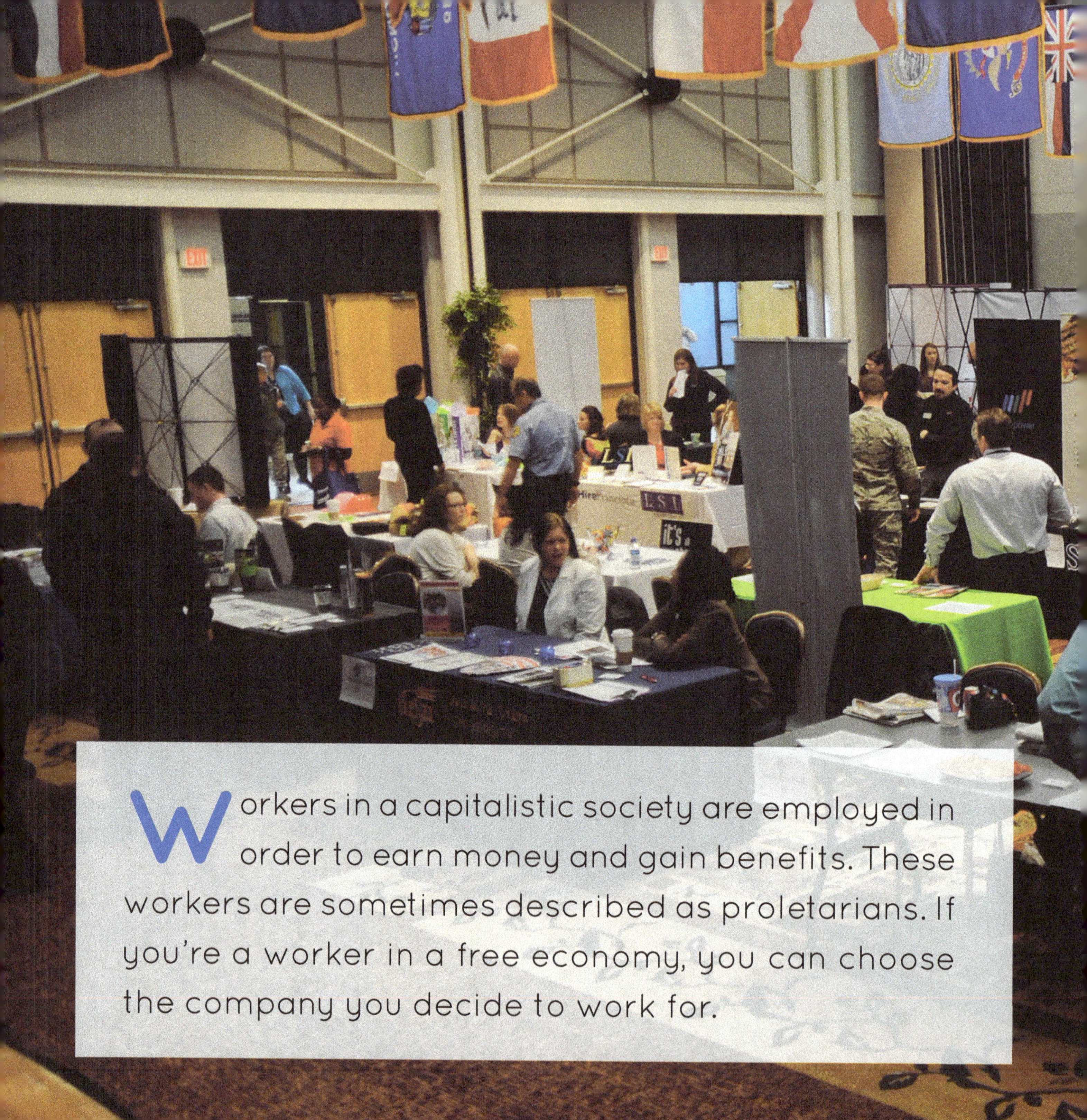

Workers in a capitalistic society are employed in order to earn money and gain benefits. These workers are sometimes described as proletarians. If you're a worker in a free economy, you can choose the company you decide to work for.

JOB FAIR

FEUDALISM

OTHER ECONOMIC SYSTEMS

In the Middle Ages, most countries had an economic system called feudalism. Individuals didn't own the land where they worked. Instead, there was a feudal lord who owned the property and the serfs were expected to pay homage to him and give him the best of their harvest before they fed themselves.

In the time of Adam Smith's writing, most European countries had a form of mercantilism. In this type of economy, nations place heavy tariffs on imports so it's difficult to trade with foreign countries.

There aren't any nations that have an ideal form of capitalism. Most capitalistic societies, including the United States, have mixed economies because they have some legal regulations in terms of what you can purchase and what you can sell. There are also rules for pricing in some cases and for how you hire employees or fire them.

In countries with mixed economies, some are more capitalist than socialist or vice versa. Socialists believe that communities not individuals should have ownership of property. They think that the production as well as the distribution of goods and services should be owned and also regulated by the community at large.

ADVANTAGES OF CAPITALISM

There are many advantages of a capitalistic economy.

CAPITALISM IS EFFICIENT.

When businesses have to compete for customers, they become more efficient.

CAPITALISM GIVES PEOPLE FREEDOM.

There is a great deal of economic freedom in a society that believes in capitalism. People on both the buying and selling side of the economy are free to do what they want.

CAPITALISM SPARKS INNOVATION.

In a society that's capitalistic, both individuals and companies receive benefits for striving for and creating new ideas and inventions. This innovation drives advances in technology faster than societies where there are no rewards for exceptional work.

CAPITALISM PROMOTES ECONOMIC GROWTH.

Capitalism has been proven to grow economies and to create a high standard of living for the citizens who live in capitalistic countries.

DISADVANTAGES OF CAPITALISM

Those who oppose capitalism highlight these weaknesses.

CAPITALISM CAN LEAD TO SOCIAL INEQUALITY.

Sometimes in a capitalistic society only a few people gain wealth and others are impoverished.

CAPITALISM CAN CREATE MONOPOLIES.

At times, companies in a capitalistic society get very large. When this happens, the company is called a monopoly.

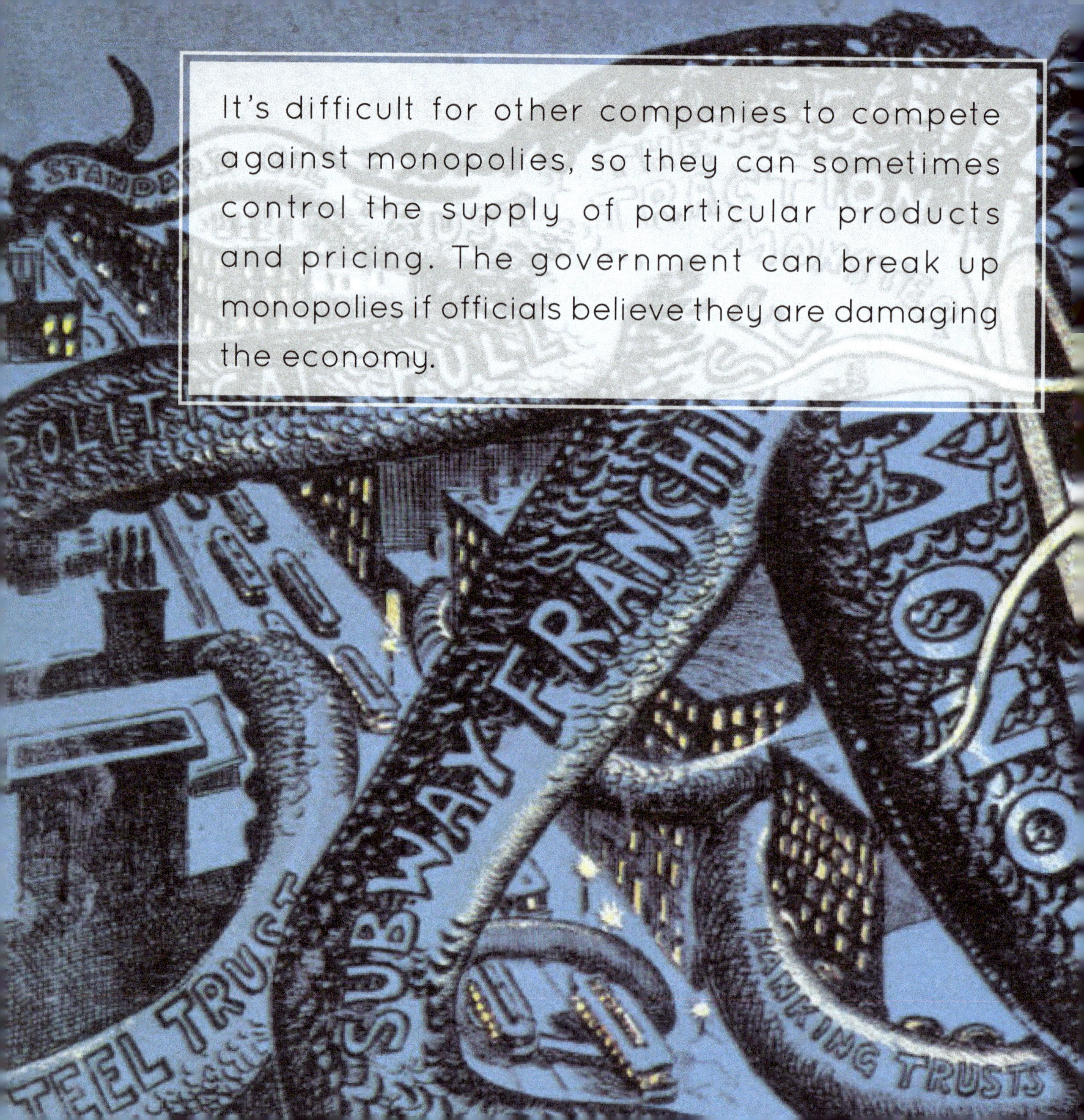

It's difficult for other companies to compete against monopolies, so they can sometimes control the supply of particular products and pricing. The government can break up monopolies if officials believe they are damaging the economy.

CAPITALISM SOMETIMES LEADS TO UNSAFE WORKING ENVIRONMENTS.

Management or owners sometimes place their workers in unsafe environments in order to make more money.

MODERN CAPITALISM

Many countries around the world have economies with capitalistic systems. However, they are different than the ideal capitalism that Adam Smith described in his book. The United States government has many regulations to ensure the economy stays stable. There are also laws to keep the public safe from fraud and keep working conditions safe.

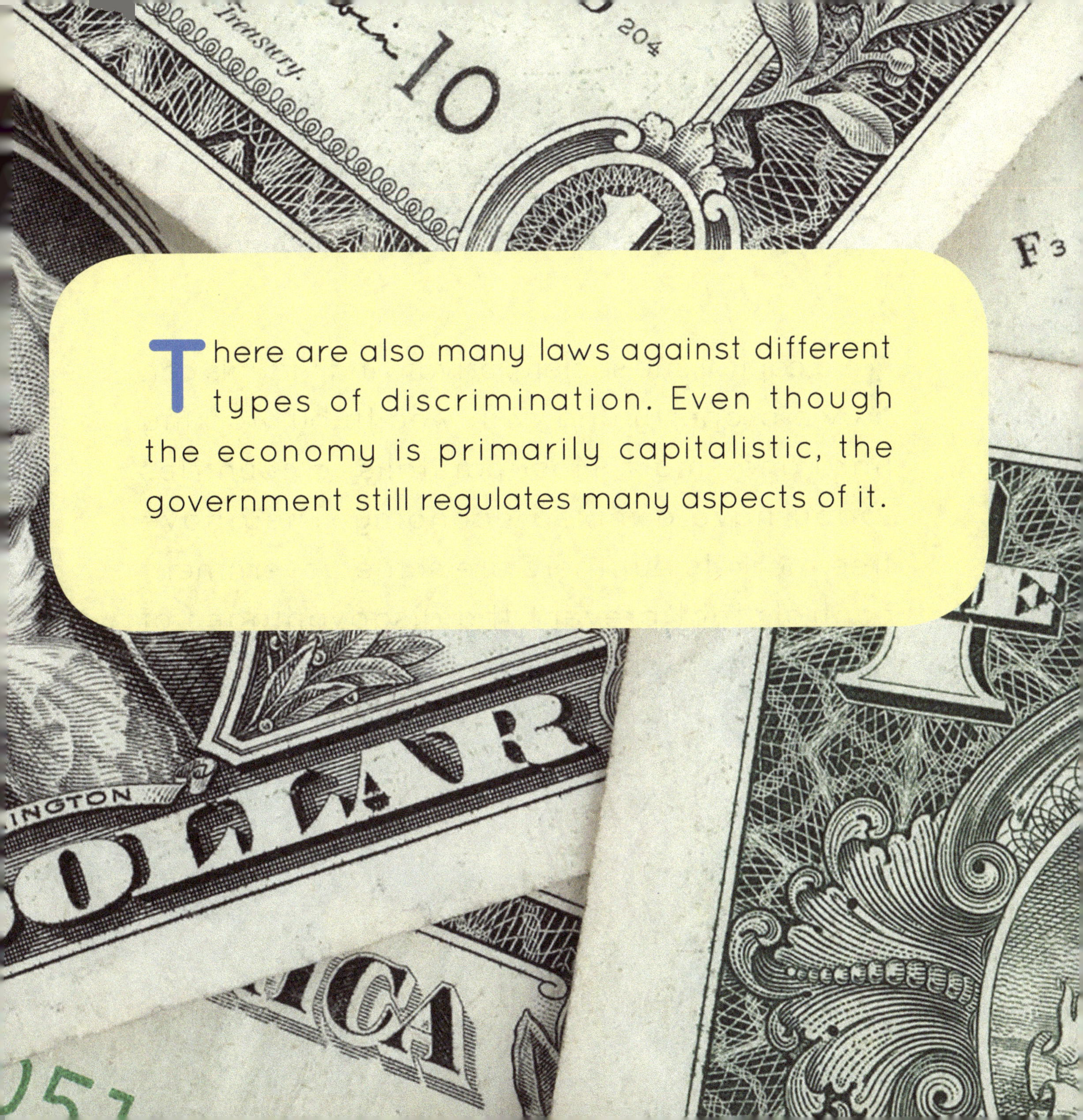

There are also many laws against different types of discrimination. Even though the economy is primarily capitalistic, the government still regulates many aspects of it.

SUMMARY

In a capitalistic society, private individuals can own property and gain wealth by working hard and smart. Most capitalistic countries today have a mixed economy. They have free markets but there are some government controls that prevent the disadvantages of capitalism such as controlling monopolies, inhumane working conditions either physical or mental, or problems with unfair earnings.

Capitalism at its best spurs economic growth as well as innovation. It also raises a nation's standard of living.

Awesome! Now that you've read about capitalism, you may want to read more about Adam Smith and his theories in the Baby Professor book Adam Smith and His Theory of the Free Market – Social Studies for Kids.

Capitalism

Visit

www.BabyProfessorBooks.com

to download Free Baby Professor eBooks
and view our catalog of new and exciting
Children's Books